EVERY DAY ON EARTH

FUN FACTS THAT HAPPEN EVERY 24 HOURS

Steve Murrie & Matthew Murrie
Illustrated by Tom Bloom

SCHOLASTIC

Acknowledgments

The authors would like to thank all of the wonderful people at Scholastic who first believed so strongly in *Every Minute on Earth* and have now been working so hard to make *Every Day on Earth* a reality. They would also like to give special thanks to the following, without whom this book (along with the rest of their books) would not have been possible: God's grace; Nancy, for her proofreading and suggestions; Seung Ah, for her patience; Dan, Holli, Libby, and Andrew, for their support; their editor, Brenda Murray, for all of her help and guidance; and their agent, Jessica Regel, for her hard work and dedication.

Text copyright © 2011 by Steve and Matthew Murrie
Illustrations copyright © 2011 by Tom Bloom
All rights reserved. Published by Scholastic Inc., *Publishers since 1920*.
SCHOLASTIC and associated logos are trademarks and/or registered trademarks of Scholastic Inc.

ISBN 978-0-545-29706-6

10 9 8 7 6 5 4 3 2 1   11 12 13 14 15

Printed in the U.S.A.   40
First edition, August 2011
Book design by Edward Miller

Contents

Introduction

Well, there goes another one. What happened? Didn't see it? Where'd it go? What on Earth are we even talking about? You were probably too busy to notice, but every day, another day goes by. You've probably heard somebody (or maybe even yourself) say "I'm counting the days" until something happens or is over. Don't believe us? How many days are left until your birthday? The holidays? The first day of school? The last day of school? Heck, if you don't have at least one day on your calendar marked, circled, or crossed out, then you're not using it right.

The only problem is, what are we doing with our days if we're just counting them down and crossing them off? Shouldn't they be more than that? *Aren't* they more than that? Imagine what would happen if, rather than counting the days that go by, you were to take note of what happened during each day. Perhaps you might find something in that day to make the day more than just a numbered box on a calendar. But how could you possibly count *everything* that happens in a single day? The Earth is a pretty big place, and there are lots of different things happening—whether we like them or not!

Counting everything that happens would be an impossible task, and it would take entire libraries of books to record everything that happened on any given day. *Every Day on Earth* is a collection of the things we thought readers would find the most mind twisting and mind blowing. Many of the facts you might even find hard to believe—or just too crazy to imagine. If this is the case, then the book has done its job.

But it is not our intention to simply hurt your head. The real purpose of this book is to get us all to become more aware of the Earth on which we reside: to take notice of its wonders, become more responsible in our interaction with it, and take care of its future. A good place to start would be to stop counting down all of the days ahead of you—trust us, there are many—and to spend more time observing and enjoying the many splendors each day holds for you and those around you. In other words: Don't count each day—make each day count!

LIVING THINGS

What do anteaters chew?

Nothing, because they don't have any teeth. Then how do they eat? With their 2-foot-long (60-centimeter) tongues! It's not impolite for anteaters to stick out their tongues, and when one does, it licks up 35,000 ants and termites in a day. These incredible creatures can flick their tongues more than 160 times a minute when catching lunch. Even though the giant anteater has 4-inch-long (10-centimeter) claws, it does not destroy the anthills or termite mounds it invades. Instead, it just opens them enough for its tongue, feeds on a few, and comes back another day for seconds.

Quick quiz: Are there more humans or kittens and puppies born every day in the United States? If you picked the pets, you passed! On an average day, 70,000 kittens and puppies are born and only 12,000 human babies are born. The most common dog breeds are the Labrador retriever, the German shepherd, and the Yorkshire terrier. The Labrador retriever has been the top dog for almost 20 years. The top cat breed is the Persian cat. Nearly 39 percent of American homes own at least one dog and 33 percent own at least one cat. There are a total of about 93.6 million pet cats and 77.5 million pet dogs living in America.

What do you call a monkey that has a mane like a male lion?

A golden lion tamarin, of course! Every day in the Brazilian rain forest about 1,500 golden lion tamarins try to survive greedy poachers and threats to their habitats. The tamarins are only 6 to 10 inches (15.2 to 25.4 centimeters) tall and weigh just 17 to 24 ounces (481.9 to 680.4 grams). A mother tamarin usually gives birth to twins, and the father and older siblings take care of the babies. Unlike most monkeys, tamarins have sharp, clawlike nails on their fingers and toes that they use to hold on to trees while climbing.

A single cow can produce around 130 gallons (500 liters) of methane gas a day.

That's enough to fill the gas tanks of 6 cars! What's behind cows' mighty burps? Cud. What is cud? It's what cows can't stop chewing. Cows live on a diet of grass or hay. After they swallow their food, it goes down into one of their four stomachs. After a while, a cow will regurgitate (spit up) its meal. This "second helping" is called cud. A cow repeats this process of chewing, swallowing, and rechewing several times. Each time its food must pass through its stomach, pockets of air are created and then released through the same end where the journey began.

Today there are only about 3,000 tigers living in the wild every day on Earth. What do you call a group of tigers? A streak! Tigers have dozens of stripes on their bodies, and no two tigers have the same pattern of stripes. No kidding. Of course, you know you shouldn't play with tigers—the large, hungry Bengal tiger can eat 60 pounds (27 kilograms) of food in one day. But did you know you should cover your ears if one looks like it's about to roar? Its roar is loud enough to be heard 2 miles (3 kilometers) away.

Did you know a plague of locusts is possible, even today?

Locusts don't look dangerous—they look more like overweight grasshoppers—but they have a habit of gathering together in large swarms (groups) that move across the land, consuming all the vegetation they can chew up. Even a small swarm can eat as much food in a day as 10 elephants, or 2,500 people! A single adult desert locust can eat its body weight of 0.07 ounce (2 grams) in food every day. Once they get hungry, locusts become very determined eaters.

In a single night's feeding, one bat can eat between 600 and 1,000 insects in one hour to be full for that day. A pregnant or nursing bat can eat as much as her own body weight in insects every day. About one-third of all bat species feed on fruit or flower nectar. This helps plants spread their seeds, which helps regenerate forests. Bats live in many diverse habitats, and they are known to pollinate all sorts of plants—from flowers in the rain forests to cactus in the deserts. But not all bats prefer fruit, flowers, and insects. A few bats feast on fish, mice, and frogs.

Who are nature's civil engineers?

Beavers, of course! They build dams and lodges using natural materials. Beaver families are very efficient at chomping down trees. A single family can chomp 300 trees in one winter, or about 3.3 trees a day! Two beavers working together can chew through a 6-inch-thick (15-centimeter) tree in just 15 minutes. Beaver dams are big and strong enough to actually change the flow of a stream. Beavers' engineering abilities are so developed, humans are the only animals who alter their environment more.

Ever wish the sun never went away?

Then you should head to either the **North or South Pole** (depending on the time of year), where there's 24 hours of daylight during the summer. If you think this sounds like a good time, you're not alone. The arctic tern sees more daylight than any other animal on the planet. The tern spends its summer months on Antarctica and, when the days start to get darker, migrates 22,000 miles (35,500 kilometers) to the **North Pole**. The tern reaches the **North Pole** in time to spend its summer there. Then it travels back to the South Pole for yet another summer.

Talk about a "whale" of an appetite.

A blue whale consumes 4 tons (3.6 metric tons) of food in a single day. A blue whale's diet is almost exclusively krill (tiny shrimplike creatures). It takes a lot of special features to allow the largest animal on Earth to eat one of the smallest. First the whale opens its extremely wide mouth, allowing thousands of gallons of krill-filled water in. The whale's giant tongue then forces the water out, trapping the krill in the meshlike strainer, called baleen, that the whale has instead of teeth. Once the krill have been separated from the water, all that's left is swallowing.

Remember in the movie *March of the Penguins* when the emperor penguins return to their rookery, where their chicks are born and raised? Quite a march. But how far do those penguins march in a day? About 5 miles (8 kilometers), which isn't very far. But that is only one day in about 2 weeks of their nearly 70-mile (110-kilometer) journey. All that waddling must be hard on the feet, huh? Not quite. These flightless birds spend most of this journey on their bellies, tobogganing across the ice instead of marching.

What's the largest bony fish in the world?

The giant sunfish! Reaching up to 4,927 pounds (2,235 kilograms), this fish also holds the world record for most eggs in vertebrates with 300 million. A 0.1-inch (2.5-millimeter) sunfish hatchling grows to 14 feet (4.2 meters) by 10 feet (3 meters)—and 60 million times its hatchling weight! That would be like you growing up to be the size and weight of six cruise ships!

How long would you sleep if you had to sleep standing up?

Maybe that's why giraffes only sleep half an hour a day—they don't lie down! A likely reason for such little shut-eye is that giraffes need to spend so much time finding the 140 pounds (65 kilograms) of food they eat every day. Their enormous size also makes them easy for predators to spot. So lying down for just a minute could turn into a permanent nap. Mothers even give birth standing up, so calves have about a 5-foot (1.5-meter) drop to the ground to welcome them into this world.

When you think of great whites, thrashing rather than traveling probably comes to mind.

But these sharks like to get away. One great white shark, named Nicole, was tagged in South Africa. Ninety-nine days later, she was observed in Western Australia, 6,897 miles (11,100 kilometers) away. Nicole traveled an average of 70 miles (112 kilometers) a day during her migration. Six months later she was found back home in South Africa. Following her journey, scientists learned that great whites can plunge to depths of 3,000 feet (900 meters). And watch out—they also found out that Nicole spent 61 percent of her time swimming just below the surface.

Imagine a bird that weighs less than one-fifth of an ounce (6.2 grams) and can fly nonstop for 500 miles (805 kilometers) in one day. The ruby-throated hummingbird accomplishes that feat every year when it flies to its winter home. The main reason it's a nonstop flight is because this bird flies over the Gulf of Mexico. The hummingbird is an omnivore, feeding mainly on flower nectar but also on tree sap from holes drilled by woodpeckers. Tasty. Amazingly, the hummingbird only consumes between 3.1 and 7.6 calories a day—that's equal to just one or two M&Ms.

If eating fungi (think mold and mushrooms) forever doesn't sound delicious, you may not be cut out to be a leaf-cutter ant. These heavyweight ants can carry leaves 6 to 10 times their weight, but they don't eat just the leaves they carry back to their underground nest. In addition, they eat the fungi that grow on them. Once the leaves are in the nest, a fast-growing fungus soon covers them as they become a part of the ants' "fungus farm." How long must the ants wait for their dinner to be ready? One day. So, every day, a new fungus forms.

What would you do if you had only a day to live?

An adult mayfly spends its single day on Earth flying around ponds and rivers. That's after having spent one full year burrowing around in mud as a slimy larva. While their life spans might be short, mayflies' numbers are large. On May 29, 2010, in La Crosse, Wisconsin, a group of mayflies hatched that was so large it showed up on the local weather station's Doppler radar as a storm over the Mississippi River.

How many eggs could you lay every day, if you could lay eggs?

If you wanted to keep up with a queen termite, you'd better get ready to get busy, because she can pop out 36,000 eggs a day! In one year she produces over 13 million eggs, and in a 15-year lifespan she'll lay about 164 million eggs (just over 13,666,666 dozen). How can you spot the queen among those millions of termites? It shouldn't be hard: Her head alone can be as large as a worker termite's body—about 0.1 inch (0.3 centimeters) to 1 inch (2.5 centimeters)—and the rest of her body can grow up to another 4 inches (11 centimeters) long. Got to have somewhere to hold all those eggs!

Every day, red pandas eat 20 to 30 percent of their body weight.

That's about 2 to 4 pounds (1 to 2 kilograms) of bamboo shoots and leaves. Which panda did Europeans learn about first, the red panda or the giant panda? In 1821 Europeans learned about the red panda, and it wasn't until 1869 that Western science was aware of the giant panda. The red panda eats mainly bamboo leaves, just like the giant panda. The red panda can spend more than 13 hours a day searching for bamboo.

Bzzzzzzzzz! Slap! Just another mosquito, but how much blood did it drink? If it was a male mosquito, none; they prefer plant juices over blood. It's the females that act like vampires in order to get enough nourishment to produce eggs. A single female mosquito drains about 0.0002 to 0.002 teaspoons (0.001 to 0.01 milliliters) of blood in a day. That means it would take between 3,000 and 30,000 mosquitoes to swallow just one ounce of blood. Scientists have found that mosquitoes sniff out their victims' smell using receptors on their antennae to pick up chemicals in human sweat.

Ever wonder why the trunk of the saguaro cactus has folds like an accordion?

These folds expand and fill up with water during rare desert rainstorms. Whenever it rains, this cactus can "drink" more than 200 gallons (760 liters) of water a day—enough to fill four bathtubs! Luckily, this daylong drink brings in enough water to last for a year. How does this cactus soak up so much water? Most of its roots are only 4 to 6 inches (10 to 15 centimeters) deep and soak up rain quickly. The saguaro starts out as a tiny seed the size of a pinhead, but it grows up to 50 feet (15 meters) and weighs 9 tons (8 metric tons).

The sandgrouse could be called the "sewing machine bird," because that's what it looks like when it's feeding.

The grouse is the busiest eater in the bird world. It will eat between 5,000 and 80,000 seeds a day, picking up several seeds a second. Another interesting feature of this bird is its special belly feathers that absorb and retain water to carry to its chicks, miles away from watering holes.

The world's smallest mammal has the fastest heartbeat of all mammals.

The heart of a pygmy shrew beats 1,728,000 times every day. But all of those beats come with a cost: The pygmy shrew also has the shortest life span of all mammals, living from 11 to 13 months. Pygmy shrews spend most of their lives looking for food and must eat something every 15 to 30 minutes, day and night. They will die if they go longer than one hour without eating.

Creature-eating plants! Sounds like science

fiction, but there are more than 500 different species of meat-eating plants on Earth. Probably the most famous is the Venus flytrap. It uses sweet-smelling nectar and steel-trap-shaped leaves to catch unfortunate insects. The flytrap has between three and six trigger hairs on each leaf. If the same hair is touched twice or if two hairs are touched within 20 seconds, the trap snaps closed. The Venus flytrap takes between 5 and 12 days to digest its prey, so in one day it will digest from one-fifth to one-twelfth of an animal, depending on its size.

What's the largest land animal on Antarctica? No,

penguins are considered marine animals because they spend most of their time at sea. No, polar bears live in the Arctic. Give up? It's the wingless midge. Reaching only 0.08 to 0.2 inches (2 to 6 millimeters) long, this tiny insect probably wouldn't fly much even if it had wings; the strong, endless winds of Antarctica would constantly overpower its flight. In one day, it may live one-tenth of its entire 10-to-14 day adult life.

Some wolf packs will travel around 50 miles (80 kilometers) every day to find their meals.

But do wolves really "wolf down" their food? Yep. One adult wolf can eat 20 pounds (9 kilograms) of food in one sitting. Wolves have inward-turning elbows, long legs, and slender bodies designed for a life on the run. Wolves also have enormous paws for their size. An average wolf track is about 4.5 inches (11 centimeters) long by 3.5 inches (9 centimeters) wide; by comparison, the only dogs with more than a 4-inch (10-centimeter) track are the Great Dane, the Saint Bernard, and a few bloodhounds.

Yuck! When a young koala stops drinking its mother's milk, the mother will give the joey (what a baby koala is called) some very soft poop called pap. An average koala will eat about 18 ounces (500 grams) of eucalyptus leaves every day. The leaves have strong toxins that must be cleansed by the koala's stomach. Eating poop while they're joeys helps koalas gradually develop the ability to detoxify their food as adults.

How many of the known 1,500 volcanoes on the Earth are erupting every day?

Only about 20 volcanoes are constantly erupting. The most famous is probably Italy's Stromboli, which has been erupting for over 2,000 years. Several volcanoes are active, which means that they *could* erupt at any given time. The active volcanoes in the United States include 40 volcanoes in the lower 48 states, 60 in Alaska, and 3 in Hawaii. Currently, the most dangerous volcano in the United States is Mount Saint Helens, in Washington, whose eruption could cause massive mudflows and swamp the valleys and plains below.

More than 100 billion aluminum cans are made each year, which means about 274 million are stamped out each day. Thanks to the recycling effort, about 40 percent of an average can is made of recycled aluminum. Recycling a can takes 95 percent less energy, creates 95 percent fewer emissions, and produces 97 percent less water pollution than making new metal from aluminum ore. Americans recycle 52 percent of all their aluminum cans, or about 141 million cans every day.

In one day, a single bacterium can grow and divide enough times to equal twice the population of New York City, producing 16 million cells! Of course, the growing conditions have to be perfect, so microbiologists use a sterile nutrient gel on a petri dish to grow the bacteria. Bacteria take different amounts of time to grow and divide. In 24 hours, a bacterium "bug" that takes one hour to do this will divide into 2 to the 24th power, or 16 million, bacteria cells.

How would you like to save 17 trees?

Recycle 1 ton (0.9 metric ton) of paper. Most families don't use a ton of paper a year, but Americans *do* receive about 11,000 tons of junk mail every day—and it all could be recycled. Recycling just a ton of paper will save about 3 cubic yards (2.3 cubic meters) of landfill space and 7,000 gallons (26,500 liters) of water used in the processing of new paper. That would save enough electricity to heat your home for half a year, while preventing an additional 60 pounds (27 kilograms) of air pollutants in the environment.

Need something to pass the time?

You could watch the grass grow. Sounds boring, but if that grass is a certain species of bamboo, you could actually see it grow. The fastest-growing bamboo can grow nearly 4 feet (1.2 meters) in one day. That's about 1.5 inches (4 centimeters) in an hour! So, if you've got an hour to watch, you could actually see a significant change. The size of full-grown bamboo can range from a couple of inches to over 100 feet (30 meters) in height with a diameter of 8 inches (20 centimeters).

Think of all the things around you that are made of cotton.

Your jeans, shirts, and socks; the sheets on your bed; the towels in your bathroom and kitchen; even your underwear. More than 133 million pounds (60.1 million kilograms) of cotton are produced around the world every day. U.S. paper money is not made of paper but of 75 percent cotton and 25 percent linen. One bale of cotton can make 215 pairs of jeans.

What's that smell? It's your turn to change the diaper. That's said more than 40,370,000 times in the United States every day. The total weight of all those disposable diapers is 1,816 tons (1,647 metric tons) going to the landfill each day. If every baby on the planet used disposable diapers, the daily use would skyrocket to 1.375 billion stinky pants a day. The United States and Mexico are number one and number two (no pun intended) in disposable diaper use.

Did you know that you have a giant in your ice cream and toothpaste?

It's the giant kelp, an alga that lives in the ocean and can grow to be 175 feet (53 meters) long. When living conditions are perfect, the giant kelp can grow 2 feet (60 centimeters) in just one day. Thousands of giant kelp can grow close together, forming a kelp forest. Sea otters like to wrap themselves up in the kelp fronds and kick back and relax. The giant kelp is a source of algin, which is a blending and binding agent that makes ice cream and toothpaste creamy.

Do you think 20,000 trees down your toilet might be a tight fit? Well,

that's about how many trees' worth of toilet paper Americans flush down their toilets every day. We better hope we don't run out of trees! Once in the wastewater system, toilet tissue is designed to break apart into small pieces and eventually decompose. The average American family of four uses almost 100 rolls of toilet paper a year! Recycled paper can be made into toilet paper, but it is slightly rougher than non-recycled paper. On the other hand, non-recycled toilet paper requires cutting down some of the Earth's oldest forests—hardly a fitting end for a 200-year-old tree.

A "glacial pace" is usually used to describe something slow moving, but that's not the case with the fastest-moving glacier on Earth.

It moves 114 feet (35 meters) every day. That's almost an inch a minute! This speeding glacier is the Jakobshavn Glacier, or Jakobshavn Isbrae (*isbrae* is Danish for "glacier"). It's located on the western coast of Greenland and is Greenland's largest outlet glacier.

One day, people will be "mining" landfills for plastic.

Most plastics take thousands of years to decompose, and if the costs of oil and natural gas keep going up, digging in landfills for plastic might become cheaper than making it. Every day, Americans throw away about 60 million plastic bottles. One company, Preserve, has a program to recycle #5 polypropylene plastic. The company recycles this plastic into toothbrushes and razor handles.

One day, in 1943, it was just a cornfield; the next day it was a fuming, spewing volcano. In one day, the Paricutín volcano rose 164 feet (50 meters) . . . and by the next week it grew to 492 feet (150 meters)! The Paricutín volcano, now 1,391 feet (424 meters) tall, is located 200 miles (321 kilometers) west of Mexico City. The volcano's hardened lava covers an area of about 10 square miles (25 square kilometers), and volcanic fragments can be found within 20 square miles (52 square kilometers). One serious eruption of Paricutín killed nearly 1,000 people in 1949.

A hurricane can spin over 155 miles (249 kilometers) per hour, but only travels between 20 and 30 miles (32 and 48 kilometers) per hour across the ocean. The average hurricane progresses between 300 and 400 miles (483 and 644 kilometers) a day and usually travels 3,000 miles (4,828 kilometers) before it finally runs out of energy and dies out. Hurricanes can be deadly, but they play an important part in cooling the Earth. Think of hurricanes as giant fans that spin the warm air above the ocean upward, where the heat escapes into the upper atmosphere and then into space.

Do icebergs move or just float in one place?

Actually, they do both. When they do travel, icebergs can do so in a zigzag line depending on their size, their shape, ocean currents, wind patterns, and waves. The fastest observed icebergs could travel about 2.2 miles per hour. That means in one day they could travel about 53 miles. Tiny air bubbles give icebergs their white color, but bubble-free icebergs have a beautiful blue tint. Greenland's glaciers calve (break away) around 110 good-sized icebergs every day, or about 40,000 every year.

Would you believe that on average lightning strikes the Earth around 8,640,000 times every day? It might be easier to believe if you traveled to Lake Maracaibo in Venezuela, where lightning strikes an average of 280 times an hour. The lightning, called Relámpago del Catatumbo, can be seen for as long as 10 hours per night during 140 to 160 nights of the year. This lightning is so clear it can be seen as far away as 200 miles (322 kilometers). If the power from just one of those lightning strikes could be harnessed for electricity, it could light up all the lightbulbs in South America for an instant.

Diamonds do not come out of the ground as bright, sparkling gems—instead, they look like semitransparent beige-colored stones.

In 2008 the world's diamond production was 165 million carats, which is about 450,000 carats recovered every day. Carats are how diamonds are measured: One carat equals 0.007 ounce (200 milligrams). Russia leads all countries in diamond production with 37 million carats and is followed by the Democratic Republic of the Congo with around 33 million carats. Out of every 1 million diamonds mined, there is only one quality 1-carat diamond recovered. It takes about 200 tons (181 metric tons) of ore to find just one diamond.

Timber! Another tree bites the dust, to be turned into lumber and other wooden products. In the United States, around 4,800,000 board feet (445,934 square meters) of lumber is produced every day—that's enough lumber to cover 1,000 American football fields without the end zones. What is a board foot? It's a wooden board that is 1 foot (30 centimeters) by 1 foot, and 1 inch (2.5 centimeters) thick. America leads the world in lumber production, but what country is second? India.

More than 51 new plant and animal species are discovered every day.

One of the most unusual is the *Nepenthes tenax*, or "rat-eating pitcher plant," discovered in Cape York, Australia. The plant normally feeds on insects, but has trapped larger animals like frogs, birds, and rats. Members of the *Nepenthes* group of pitcher plants are also called "monkey cups" because monkeys have been seen using the plants to drink out of like pitchers.

When you look at the ocean, you see the waves coming in one at a time, but what you don't see are the strong ocean currents.

The fastest ocean currents can carry the shallow seawater between 75 and 80 miles (120 and 129 kilometers) a day. Deep ocean currents don't have the wind helping as much and usually travel only about 5 miles (8 kilometers) a day.

Where do plastic bags come from?

Plastic bags are made from crude oil, natural gas, and other petrochemicals. Unfortunately, about 273,972,603 plastic bags are thrown away every day in America. That's almost one bag per person in the United States! Even worse, Americans recycle less than 1 percent of their plastic bags. Recently, Ireland enacted a bag tax, which caused a 95 percent reduction in plastic bag use throughout the country.

Which one is real: Captain Jack, the ship *Black Pearl*, or the black pearl?

It's the black pearl, one of the most sought-after pearls in all the Earth. It is 100 times rarer than the white pearl. Oddly enough, black pearls aren't always black. They can be sea green, emerald green, dark green, indigo, cranberry, or a deep midnight black. The giant black-lipped oyster can take two to five years to produce a black pearl. Not all pearls take so long; more than 4 tons (3.6 metric tons) of the more common freshwater pearls are produced every day in China alone.

If you could make an extremely loud sound, could it travel around the world in one day?

Sound can travel through the air at around 761 miles (1,217.6 kilometers) per hour, or 18,264 miles (29,393 kilometers) every day. The Earth's circumference is 24,860 miles (40,008 kilometers) around the poles and 24,901 miles (40,075 kilometers) around the equator, so the sound would travel about three-quarters of the way around the Earth. If you were at the North Pole, you could make a humongous sound that would travel south all the way to the South Pole and then back to the equator in one day.

Did you know that the United States has a national tree? Is it the redwood, the maple, the pine, the dogwood, or the oak? If you guessed oak, you're correct. A nationwide vote was hosted by the Arbor Day Foundation; the oak was the top vote-getter. Congress passed a bill designating the oak as our national tree and former President George W. Bush signed the bill. There are more than 60 kinds of oak growing in the United States, and they are prized for their beauty, shade, and lumber. Every year, members of the Arbor Day Foundation plant an average of 22,000 trees a day.

FOOD

An apple a day keeps the doctor away.

This might be true, but apples may do a better job in keeping the dentist away because of their teeth-cleaning effect. Americans consume around 685,000 bushels (2.4 million liters) of apples and apple products every day. This means the average American consumes an estimated 16.9 pounds (7.7 kilograms) of apples each year.

Pass the juice, please! In most American homes, *juice* means orange juice. About three out of four households in America buy orange juice each trip to the supermarket. Almost 49 million pounds (22 million kilograms) of Florida oranges are squeezed into orange juice every day. At one time, oranges were considered a luxury; to get an orange in a Christmas stocking in the middle of winter was an incredible treat. Today, having an orange any time of the year is not as big a deal. Florida produces the most oranges in the United States, with about 96 percent of its oranges squeezed into juice.

The Oreo cookie has been called the all-American cookie.

It's hard to believe, but the Oreo was first introduced in 1912 as the Oreo Chocolate Sandwich Cookie. It's still a mystery how it got its name; one rumor is that it comes from the French word for gold, *or*, because its first package was gold colored.

The breakdown of an Oreo is 71 percent cookie and 29 percent creme filling. More than 20 million Oreos are eaten every day. If you could assemble all the Oreos ever made, they would circle the equator 381 times and if stacked, they could reach the moon five times over.

What is maize?

It's another word for corn. And you'd be *amazed* at how much is produced in the United States: on average, more than 1.9 billion pounds (842 million kilograms) every day! Corn is used in making food—for humans and animals—and even alcohol fuel for cars. Corn is also used to decorate a palace. Every year, the Corn Palace in Mitchell, South Dakota, is covered in murals made of corn and other grains. The palace also hosts a popular rodeo, but they have to be careful all those horses don't eat the art!

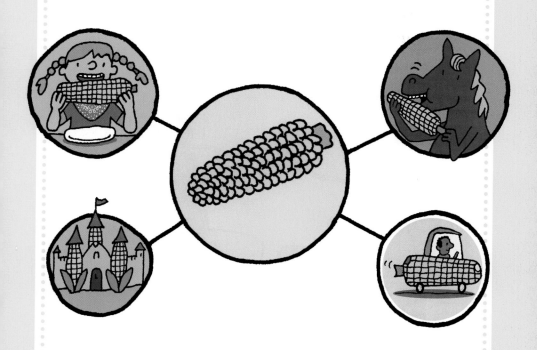

Just about everyone likes pasta; it's one of America's most popular foods.

The United States produces almost 1.9 million tons (1.7 million metric tons) a year, or more than 10 million pounds (4.5 million kilograms) a day! Sounds like a lot, until you consider the Italians, who make 2.75 million tons (2.5 million metric tons) of pasta each year—and they have one-fifth the population of the United States. There are more than 600 different shapes of pasta made around the world. Pasta can be colored green (spinach added), red (tomatoes added), or black or gray (squid ink added), and some is even transparent when cooked.

Can you imagine trading a piece of gold for potatoes?

That's what happened during the Alaskan Klondike gold rush in 1897–1898 when hungry miners wanted something good to eat. Today, potato chips are the favorite snack food of Americans, who down over 3 million pounds (15 million kilograms) every single day. The potato chip has been around since 1853, when Saratoga Springs chef George Crum came up with the idea while trying to please some finicky diners. The diners thought the potato slices were too thick, so Chef Crum sliced them as thin as he could. The diners loved them, and the potato chip was invented.

The early American colonists' recipe for pumpkin pie: Cut off the pumpkin top; remove seeds; fill with milk, honey, and spices; then place in hot ashes for a few hours to bake. Pumpkins are native to the Americas. Pumpkins grow on ground-hugging vines that can grow more than 6 inches (15 centimeters) a day during their peak growth spurt. Each pumpkin plant produces male and female flowers. The flowers are the same color, but the male flowers grow on long stems, are the first to bloom, and are more plentiful. The female flowers grow closer to the main vine and produce the pumpkin.

What's the most popular candy bar?

Here are some hints: 15 million are made each day, 99 tons (90 metric tons) of peanuts are used daily to make them, and each bar contains about 16 peanuts. It's the Snickers bar. Frank Mars, founder of the candy company Mars, Incorporated, was the creator of the Snickers bar. How did he come up with the name? He named it after one of his favorite horses. The first candy bar sold by Mars, Incorporated, was the Milky Way, which was the brainchild of Frank's son, Forrest. The Snickers bar was the company's second candy bar.

Why is it called Gatorade? Is it made from

alligator parts? Nope. Gatorade, the most popular sports drink in the United States, was developed at the University of Florida for their Florida Gators football team. When you sweat during exercise, your body doesn't just lose water. It loses important electrolytes, sodium and potassium, as well. Sports drinks have water fortified with sodium and potassium to help replace what you lose. More than 2.5 million gallons (9.5 million liters) of Gatorade were consumed every day in 2009.

Each Thanksgiving Day in the United States, more than 45 million turkeys are cooked and consumed.

That accounts for one-sixth of all the turkeys eaten each year. All those turkeys combined weigh about 675 million pounds (306 million kilograms), and if you divide that number by the 310 million people in the United States, it means the average person is eating more than 2.2 pounds (1 kilogram) of Thanksgiving turkey. That includes leftovers!

Let us eat more lettuce.

In fact, Americans are eating five times more lettuce than they did in the early 1900s. Today a typical American eats nearly 30 pounds (13 kilograms) of lettuce a year, which averages to 1.3 ounces (35 grams) every day. Lettuce ranks second behind the potato as the most popular fresh vegetable in the United States. More than 73 percent of all lettuce produced is iceberg lettuce; however, romaine lettuce, with its darker leaves, is more nutritious. Lettuce was considered a weed before people in the Mediterranean started using it as food. We can thank Christopher Columbus for bringing lettuce to the New World.

Can you believe that a lemon tree can produce 1,500 lemons a year?

That's an average of a little more than four lemons every day! All those lemons would weigh between 500 and 600 pounds (227 and 272 kilograms). Lemon trees bloom all year long, and their lemons can be picked more than six times in a year. India and Mexico are the largest producers of lemons in the world. California and Arizona produce more than 90 percent of all lemons in the United States. Catholic missionaries were the first to plant lemons in California and Arizona.

Can a candy company make 1 million miles (1.6 million kilometers) of candy a year?

More than 1 million miles of Twizzlers are made every year. That's enough to stretch to the moon and back to the Earth two times! It also means about 2,740 miles are made every day. The Y&S plant in Lancaster, Pennsylvania, made the world's largest Twizzler. It was 1,200 feet (366 meters) long and weighed 100 pounds (45 kilograms)! Twizzlers is a licorice-based candy that had its beginning in 1845 by Y&S Candies. Licorice is made from the licorice root. This root contains a compound that is almost 50 times sweeter than sugar.

Mushrooms are being produced in the United States at a rate of about 2.3 million pounds (1 million kilograms) a day. The annual per capita consumption for most Americans is 4 pounds (1.8 kilograms), but for Asian Americans it's 9 pounds (4 kilograms). The Japanese lead the world in annual per capita consumption with 26 pounds (11.8 kilograms).

Chocolate chip cookies are the second most eaten cookie in the United States, just behind Oreos.

Every day, millions of packages of chocolate chips are made in the United States. The chocolate chip cookie began in 1930, at the Toll House Inn. Ruth Wakefield, the co-owner, was making her Butter Drop Do cookies when she noticed she was out of baker's chocolate, so she put in pieces of a semisweet chocolate bar instead. Her guests loved the cookies and word spread to the Nestlé chocolate company. They made a deal with Ruth: The Toll House recipe would be on their package, and she would get a lifetime supply of chocolate chips.

1930

Walnuts are one of the most nutritious nuts on Earth. Unlike many of the foods we eat, which have been brought to America from other countries, the black walnut is native to America. More than 65 percent of all black walnuts are produced in the state of Missouri. The meat of the black walnut is put in food products, and its shell is hard enough to be used in abrasives. California supplies a whopping 99 percent of the U.S. supply of English walnuts with about 2.4 million pounds (1.1 million kilograms) produced every day.

How would you like to travel across the Atlantic Ocean with a hive full of bees?

That's how the early colonists brought bees to the New World. Honey is created when bees mix flower nectar with their bee enzymes. Honey can have many different flavors and colors depending on the kind of nearby flowers and the climate of the area. Bees in America produce almost 400,000 pounds (181,000 kilograms) of honey every day. Sweet!

A single bee only lives 45 days and produces just about one-quarter of a teaspoon (1.2 milliliters) of honey in its lifetime.

Coco, or "monkey face," is what the early Spanish explorers called the coconut, because the three indentations and the hairy nut looked like the face and head of a monkey. The coconut can be used to make food, drinks, fuel, fiber, musical instruments, and utensils, along with many other items. Coconuts are important to about one-third of the world's population for their nutrtional value and their role in the economy. More than 300 million pounds (136 million kilograms) are produced every day.

Have you had 2 ounces (60 milliliters) of ice cream or frozen dairy product today? If you have, you're an average American ice-cream consumer. The North Central states eat about twice that much, making their residents the country's largest consumers. The biggest ice cream–loving cities are Portland, Oregon, and St. Louis, Missouri. Kids from 2 to 12 eat the most ice cream, and July and August are when most ice cream is consumed. Vanilla is the favorite flavor, followed by chocolate. In 1983 Cookies 'n' Cream was introduced and became the fastest-growing new flavor in ice-cream history.

What's the most consumed fruit or vegetable in the United States?

It's the tomato (a fruit). More than 77 million pounds (35 million kilograms) are eaten daily, which is about one-quarter of a pound (113 grams) for each American. It's believed that the Aztecs and Incas were the first to cultivate tomatoes. Early explorers brought tomatoes back to Europe, where they were written about in 1556. There are more than 7,000 different kinds of tomatoes.

Who brought sugarcane to the New World?

In 1493, Columbus brought sugar to you and me. The United States produces about 1.6 billion pounds (726 million kilograms) of sugarcane-made sugar every year. That's about 4.4 million pounds (2 million kilograms) a day. Because it needs little fertilizer and pesticide, sugarcane is one of nature's most environmentally friendly crops. A sugarcane company in Maui, Hawaii, even burns the leftover sugarcane residue to generate electricity for the plant processing the sugarcane. The excess electricity they produce supplies between 7 and 8 percent of all of Maui's homes and businesses.

Beans, beans, the musical fruit, the more you eat, the more you . . . you know the rest. That verse is right on two levels: Beans are the seeds of plants, and botanically speaking, a fruit. Beans also contribute to the production of flatulence (gas) in people. More than a million tons of beans are grown in the United States every year, about 5.4 million pounds (2.4 million kilograms) a day.

Would you eat a "little donkey"? The

word *burrito* means "little donkey" in Spanish. No one knows
for sure when the burrito came about, but there are plenty of
stories. One story is that during the Mexican Revolution, taco-
stand owner Juan Mendez decided to wrap his taco ingredients
in a flour tortilla to keep them warm. Juan's wrap was a huge
success. Every day, Chipotle Mexican Grill serves about
700,000 people their burritos, and they use about 191,780.8
pounds (86,990.3 kilograms) of meat to do so.

Whether you call them sliders or belly bombers, hamburger aficionados know what you're talking about: White Castle hamburgers. White Castle got its start in Wichita, Kansas, in 1921, under Walter A. Anderson and Edgar Waldo "Billy" Ingram. If there were a hamburger hall of fame, Anderson would be a shoo-in for enshrinement: not only did he help build the Castle, he also created the hamburger bun. White Castle was the first fast-food restaurant to sell a million hamburgers and later, the first to sell a billion. On an average day, White Castle serves over 1.37 million sliders.

More than 39.2 million pounds (17.8 million kilograms) of tortilla chips were bought every day in the two weeks preceding the 2009 Super Bowl XLV. That's more than 2.8 million pounds (1.3 million kilograms) a day! The first tortilla chips were made in Los Angeles when Rebecca Webb Carranza's new tortilla-making machine produced misshapen tortillas. Instead of throwing away the misshaped pieces, Carranza cut them into triangles and fried them. They were called Tort Chips, and by the 1960s they were a widespread hit. Ms. Carranza went on to receive the Golden Tortilla award from the Mexican food industry.

When you think of your favorite "comfort food," what comes to mind? While everyone might have a different list, one food tends to show up on more lists than any other: macaroni and cheese. In 2009 Americans bought more than $802 million of mac and cheese. That means they were probably eating about 2.2 million boxes of the good stuff every day. The first credited recipe for mac and cheese is from Mrs. Elizabeth Raffald in 1769.

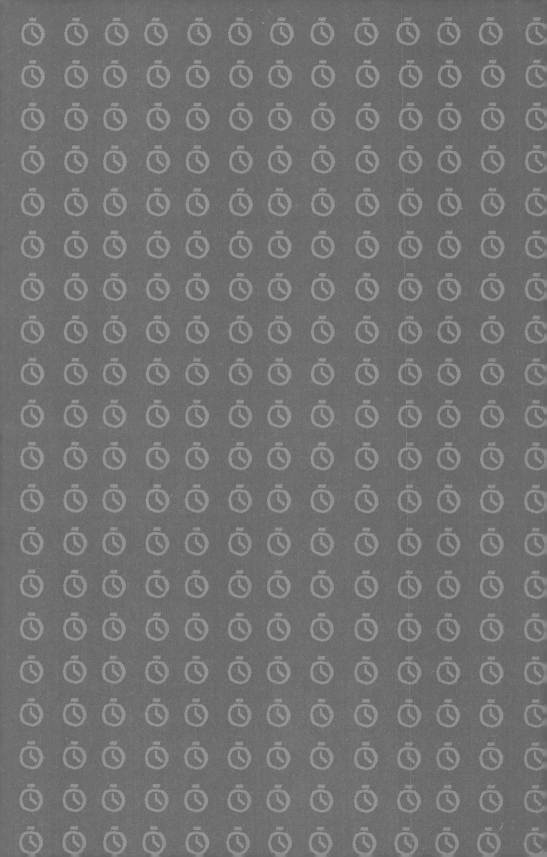

THE HUMAN BODY

What's the most misunderstood product of the human body?

Have you heard of bile? You can use the word to describe an angry person, but your liver produces between 3.4 cups and 1 quart (800 to 1,000 milliliters) of it every day to help keep you alive. Where does your body store all that bile? In your gallbladder. What's bile made of? Bile is made of water, bile salts, cholesterol, and phospholipids. What does it do? Bile helps break down fats; provides a means for vitamins A, D, E, and K to be absorbed by the body; and helps regulate cholesterol.

What process is happening deep inside your bones every minute of every day—even while you're sleeping?

The marrow of your bones is busy making billions of red blood cells, white blood cells, and platelets every day. The red blood cells live about 120 days, the platelets survive about 10 days, and the various kinds of white blood cells can last anywhere from a few days to years. Altogether, the human body works to make about 24 billion new cells a day.

How much of your body is made of water?

A healthy adult is made up of about 60 percent water, but a baby is around 80 percent water; maybe that's why babies pee a lot. An average male adult should consume 13 cups (3 liters) of water every day and an adult female should have about 9 cups (2.1 liters). Not that thirsty? Don't sweat. You don't have to actually *drink* that much, because foods like fruits and vegetables contain water that can count toward your total water intake. Where does the water go? Your body gets rid of it in a variety of ways, the most obvious being the about 6.3 cups (1.5 liters) you pee every day.

Tears—they're not just for crying anymore. Your lachrymal (tear)

glands are producing 2 to 3 ounces (59 to 89 milliliters) of tears a day. You might think of tears as being just water, but they're not; tears mix with oil and mucus from other glands as they move across your eyes. Tears are designed to cleanse, nourish, and lubricate the eyeball. Because the cornea lacks blood vessels, it relies on tears to provide it with nutrients and allow oxygen to be absorbed from the air. Excess tears drain through two holes and eventually end up in your nose or in the back of your throat. That's why your nose runs when you cry.

Who burns fat faster, men or women?

Men burn 50 more fat calories a day than women burn. Scientists believe this is true because women require a higher basic body fat proportion than men due to their role in reproduction. This extra fat tissue helps cushion developing babies, and the fat reserves help mothers and babies survive if there is a period of very little or no food to eat. Scientists have observed that muscle tissue burns between 7 and 10 calories per pound (0.45 kilogram) per day and fat tissue will burn only 2 to 3 calories per pound (0.45 kilogram) a day.

Dream on. Most of us do dream—about five times during **REM** (Rapid Eye Movement) sleep to be exact. During **REM** sleep, your eyes move back and forth very quickly. When they woke subjects during **REM** sleep, sleep scientists noticed that the subjects reported having been woken from a dream. Luckily, during **REM** sleep, the brain slows muscle activity so that we do not act out our dreams. Can you imagine enacting a sword fight while you dream? One thing you cannot do during **REM** is sleepwalk.

Air doesn't weigh much, right? However, every day the adult human breathes in 88 pounds (40 kilograms) of air (the average weight of a 10-year-old child). In an average day, without running a marathon or doing other strenuous exercise, a person breathes in about 1.6 gallons (6 liters) of air each minute and takes 24,000 breaths. This means that the average adult breathes in 2,282 gallons (8,640 liters) of air daily. Breathing is the body's number-one way of getting rid of waste: 70 percent by breathing, 20 percent through skin, 7 percent with urine, and 3 percent with feces.

Would you believe that in one day your heart pumps enough blood to fill the tank of a fire engine? Yep, your heart pumps about 2,000 gallons (7,570 liters) of blood in just 24 hours. An adult heart only weighs between 8 and 10 ounces (227 and 284 grams) and is about the size of two fists. Maybe more amazing is the fact that your body has more than 60,000 miles (96,561 kilometers) of blood vessels—capillaries, veins, and arteries. It only takes 20 seconds for blood to make a complete trip around the circulatory system.

Imagine trying to count the number of times a six-year-old laughs in a day.

Sound impossible? Just in case you lost count, the average six-year-old laughs 300 times a day! How does that compare to adults? An adult typically laughs just 15 to 100 times a day. For adults, laughing 100 times a day burns the same number of calories as cycling for 15 minutes. So people who "lighten up" might also be lightening in weight. Laughter is a sound recognized by people from all over the world, making laughter a universal language.

Riddle time: I'm about the size of a computer mouse.

You have two of me in your body, but can live with just one of me. I'm made of more than a million microscopic parts. Give up? I'm a kidney. Every day, blood filters through your kidneys more than 400 times! During that time, your kidneys filter about 47 gallons (178 liters) of blood. In addition to producing urine, the kidneys' main purpose is to keep the correct balance of water and minerals in your body. Kidneys even produce a hormone that tells your body to make more red blood cells.

Ever wonder why there are more bald men than women?

Men lose nearly 40 hairs every day, but women drop 70 hairs daily! Women start out with more hair *and* they grow lost hair back more than men. Also, some men are just born with genes that destine them for permanent hair loss. Hair growth goes through a two- to three-year cycle, during which 90 percent of a person's hair is growing and the remaining 10 percent is in a resting stage. The resting hair falls out in three to four months and new hair takes its place.

Did you know that you smell "in stereo"?
Each nostril sends the scent signal to different parts of the brain. This helps you tell the direction and the source of the odor. You might take the sense of smell for granted, but it's a very complex and important sense. There are about 10 million scent receptors on the upper surface of your nasal passage working for you every day. Thousands of different odors can be distinguished by these sensitive receptors.

Do you think a snake is the only living thing that sheds its skin? It's

not. When a snake sheds its skin, it sheds it all, even the scales that covered its eyes at one time. But people are shedding their skin little by little every day, with a daily total of 72 million skin cells shed per person! About every 27 days, humans shed and regrow their epidermis, or outer layer of skin. In an average person's lifetime, they'll have grown almost 1,000 new skins.

Drool, dribble, slobber, spittle, and spit are all names for saliva. Humans produce 1 to 3 pints (473 to 1,419 milliliters) of saliva every day. Saliva is 98 percent water and contains electrolytes, mucus, enzymes, and antibacterial agents. Saliva has a digestive enzyme, amylase, that starts digesting starchy foods in the mouth even before they get to the stomach. One function of saliva is to protect the teeth when a person vomits. Good thing, too, because vomit contains very acidic stomach chemicals that can eat away at teeth.

Who "cut the cheese"? You mean, who passed gas? Everyone does . . . an average of 14 times a day. The total volume of the daily gas passed is between 1 and 4 pints (473 to 1892 milliliters). Your gas has two possible exits: burped out of your mouth, or out the other end! Most of the gases involved in your flatulence—carbon dioxide, oxygen, nitrogen, hydrogen, and some methane—are odorless. That obnoxious odor comes from gases containing sulfur, produced by bacteria in the large intestine.

Can you feel your stomach moving?

Most people can at some time feel stomach movement, but can you feel the muscles in your small intestine (gut) move? They're contracting and relaxing 12 to 16 times a minute, working to break up the large chunks of food that come from the stomach into smaller pieces. At the same time, the muscle contractions move the food through the length of the small intestine, where most of the nutrients are absorbed into the body, to the large intestine. In one day, the muscles of the small intestine make around 20,000 contractions, known as peristalsis.

Have you ever tried to count the number of steps you take in a day?

If your number is around 8,000 (couch potatoes take about 3,000), then you're taking the average number of steps daily. If not, you'd better step it up. Doctors recommend people take 10,000 steps every day to stay fit. Professional racewalker Tim Seaman is the U.S. indoor 5-kilometer (3-mile) champion, having walked that distance in 19 minutes, 21 seconds, and 56 milliseconds. Walking involves the use of 200 of the 640 or so muscles in your body. But walking doesn't just work out your legs and feet: It gives your abdominal (tummy) muscles a workout as well.

Have you ever noticed that when you walk barefoot on cold tile, you leave footprints on them? The "moisture footprints" you leave behind are made by the sweat glands on the bottoms of your feet. People lose about 2 cups (0.5 liter) of sweat from those glands every day. That's easy to understand when you realize that each foot has about 250,000 sweat glands; that's half a million for each pair of feet. The sole of the foot has the greatest concentration of sweat glands in the body (your back has the least). Who has more sweat glands—men or women? Women.

Would you believe that you have taste buds in your cheeks, throat, and even on the roof of your mouth?

A young person has about 8,000 taste buds, and within each taste bud there are about 100 taste receptor cells, each with a very short life span. Around 100,000 of the taste receptor cells in your mouth are replaced every day. News flash! The taste map of the tongue showing the locations of the four basic tastes is wrong! All parts of the tongue are able to taste each taste. By the way, scientists have discovered a new taste called umami—the featured taste in bacon, miso, and Parmesan cheese.

The human body is a chemical factory, and one of the strongest chemicals it produces is hydrochloric acid, or HCl.

HCl is strong enough to dissolve some metals! The stomach produces around 2 quarts (1.89 liters) of the acid HCl every day. The acid helps digest food and creates an environment in which digestive enzymes can work at their best. The stomach acid also kills many of the bacteria that people ingest in their food. The stomach has the ability to expand to 3.5 quarts (3.3 liters), although this rarely happens unless you're a competitive eater.

How many times do you think in a day?

On an average day the brain will come up with an estimated 70,000 thoughts. Your brain has the power to handle all of those thoughts because it has about 100 billion nerve cells (neurons). That's about the number of stars in the **Milky Way** galaxy! One human brain can produce more electrical signals in one day than all the phone calls in the world. Your brain uses 20 percent of the body's energy but is only 2 percent of the body's weight. The amount of blood that passes through the brain every minute would fill three soda cans.

I've got to pee!

Why do humans have to pee so much? Maybe it's because your body is making urine (pee) 24/7. Most people produce from 3.3 to 8.5 cups (800 to 2000 milliliters) of urine a day. Your kidneys are constantly filtering waste and impurities out of the blood, and the result of this filtering is your urine. Want to give your urine a new scent? Eat asparagus and within 15 to 30 minutes your urine with smell very different. Thirsty? One company in India is making a soft drink from cow urine called *gau jai*, which means "cow water." Mmm.

Superhero cells? Your body's got them. They spring into action whenever "evildoers" break through your body's outer defenses. They're your white blood cells, or leukocytes, and they attack dangerous invaders using several "superweapons." Even though they make up only 1 percent of your blood, there can be as many as 7,000 to 25,000 in a single drop. The number of white blood cells can double within one day in response to an infection. The life cycle of a typical white blood cell is short: from a few days to a few weeks. But these cells are constantly being made to "fight for truth, justice, and your body's healthy way."

Are you talking to me?
Would you believe that most people spend 70 to 80 percent of each day communicating? How about that 70 percent of communication is done without using words? How's that possible? Most people rely more heavily on nonverbal communication (gestures, facial expressions, and posture, for example) than on spoken words. What about words? The average person speaks right around 16,000 words (16,215 for women, 15,669 for men) every day.

Most world languages have more than 50,000 words, but in everyday speaking people use the same few hundred words. In total, there are around 6,000 to 7,000 world languages. More than half of the world's population can speak two or more languages. There are more than 130 different languages spoken in Russia alone!

POP CULTURE

What would people do without their phone apps? Over 1 billion apps were downloaded in the first nine months they were available from Apple's iTunes; that's 3,703,703 downloads a day! The one billionth app was called Bump. It enabled two iPhone users to download information from one phone to the other by bumping their phones together. As of June 2010, the total number of app downloads is more than 5 billion. New apps are being developed at an average rate of more than 309 every day.

Guess what's the latest bicycle craze?

It's bike-sharing programs, which allow people to rent a bicycle from a public station in large cities around the world. Paris, France, has one of the most successful programs with 20,000 bikes, 1,500 bike stations, and 3 million people in the program. Nice Ride Minnesota is the largest bike-share in the United States, with 700 bikes and 65 stations in Minneapolis, which was named the most bike-friendly city in the United States. With almost 300,000 bikes made every day, the bike-share program is an excellent way of getting bikes to people who need them and don't want to keep and maintain them at home.

How quickly can you become a Web star?

Just ask Greyson Chance. One day he's playing the piano and singing "Paparazzi" in a talent show for his middle school in Edmond, Oklahoma. Then his singing performance is posted on YouTube. Within two months the video went viral. So far it has gotten over 37 million views, or about 210,000 hits a day. Chance has also written his own songs: "Stars," "Broken Hearts," and "Waiting Outside the Lines." They've been posted on YouTube as well, receiving more than 4, 7, and 2 million hits respectively.

Who hasn't heard of Facebook? With more than 600 million users, Facebook ranks as the largest social network in the world. Since Facebook was founded in February 2004, about 234,834 people have joined it every day. Facebook was the brainchild of Mark Zuckerberg when he was in college. It was inspired by an actual book in which students in Mark's high school recorded information about themselves to share with classmates. In April 2008, Facebook surpassed the MySpace social network in unique monthly worldwide visitors. Facebook receives about 500 million people visiting its site each month.

Why don't you Google it? The

word *Google* has taken the place of the word *search*.
Every day there are more than 3 *billion* searches
on the Internet. What exactly is a google? Actually,
it's a wordplay on *googol*, which is the number 1
followed by 100 zeroes. Every day, Google receives
search requests from every continent on the planet.
And it can search for information in 45 non-English
languages. More than 8,000 "Googlers" work at
the Googleplex in Mountain View, California, to keep
things Googling smoothly.

In 1917, Girl Scouts in Muskogee, Oklahoma, launched the very first Girl Scout Cookie campaign. Back then,

the Girl Scouts actually baked their own cookies and sold them in their school cafeteria as a service project. Now, during the cookie-selling season, Girl Scouts sell more than 3 million boxes of cookies a day. The biggest sellers are the Thin Mints. Two million of these favorites are made daily in an oven as long as a football field.

Look, he's riding a Hog! *Hog* is a nickname

for a Harley-Davidson motorcycle. The nickname dates back to the 1920s, when one Harley racing team had a pig as the team's mascot. When they won a race, they'd take a victory lap with the pig on their motorcycle. William Harley and Arthur and Walter Davidson produced the first Harley-Davidson motorcycle in 1903. In 1905, they produced a total of 8 motorcycles. Today, the 9,000 employees of the Harley-Davidson Motor Company make around 822 motorcycles a day.

They make hamsters with artificial intelligence? Yep, they're

called Zhu Zhu Pets and they're one of the most popular toys on the market. During the 2009 fall holiday and Christmas seasons, between 11,000 and 13,500 Zhu Zhu Pets were made every day. What's not to like about them? They're the world's first interactive, realistic plush AI toy hamsters. When in the nurturing mode they will coo and purr, and in the adventure mode they will buzz around the room making audio and mechanical reactions to different habitat situations.

How many times did you text today?

If you didn't send more than 17 texts, you're falling behind! The average is 17 texts a day in the United States. In 2005, the average number of text messages was just 3.3 per person every day. However, today many of the text messages are pictures, videos, and other multimedia items that some of the early phones lacked the capacity to capture and send. By the way, the official name for a text message is Short Message Service (SMS).

Taylor Swift, an outsider? At age 12, Taylor
wrote "The Outsider" because she felt like a total outcast in
her school. It was one of the first of over 200 songs she has
written. Taylor was 14 when she signed a publishing deal with
Sony/ATV, making her their youngest published songwriter
ever. Taylor also went on to become the youngest artist to win
Entertainer of the Year at the 2009 Country Music Awards. In its
first week of release, her second album, *Fearless*, sold 592,000
copies. That's about 84,571 copies every day that week!

Buy a pair and someone else gets one free.

When American traveler Blake Mycoskie was traveling through Argentina in 2006, he noticed many children did not have shoes to wear. Back home, he created the TOMS Shoes company and instituted a program called One for One. For every pair of shoes purchased in the United States, TOMS would give a needy child a pair of shoes. Later in 2006, Blake and family, friends, and staff returned to Argentina with 10,000 pairs of shoes. TOMS has given away over 1 million pairs of shoes since 2006, which averages out to about 587 pairs of shoes given away each day.

What comes out at Twilight? Just millions
of moviegoers! The opening weekend for the movie *Twilight*
saw ticket sales of $23 million a day! And that was just in the
United States. The latest movie in the Twilight series, *Eclipse*,
had similar gross receipts of about $69 million for its opening
weekend. More Twilight movies are on the way. Yes, *movies*—
the fourth and final book, *Breaking Dawn*, is going to be split
into two different movies with the first being released in
November 2011.

What's wrong with tap water?

Nothing, but Americans spend more than $100 billion every year on bottled water and drink almost 24 million gallons (91 million liters) of bottled water every day. More bottled water is sold than milk, fruit beverages, sports drinks, or coffee. Only carbonated soft drinks outsell bottled water. Studies have shown that tap water is usually cleaner than bottled water. Making the plastic bottles uses 1.5 million barrels of oil annually, which could fuel about 100,000 cars for an entire year.

Snakes on a plane? Not really, but there was a

rattlesnake found in luggage at the Unclaimed Baggage Store,
located in Scottsboro, Alabama. Every day, this store displays
around 7,000 newly arrived items from airports' unclaimed
baggage. In one suitcase, a small plastic bag had a tiny rock that
turned out to be a 40-carat natural emerald. Other finds have
included an entire suit of armor, a mummified Egyptian falcon,
and a shrunken head. A neatly folded parachute was also found,
probably in the carry-on bag of someone who was afraid of
flying—but not skydiving.

What's the latest exercise craze?

It involves moving a magic wand in front of a **TV** screen.
Nintendo's **Wii** consoles and programs have taken over the
world with their interactive full-body, motion-sensitive wireless
controllers, and video games. In December 2009, more than
122,903 **Wii** consoles were sold every day, thanks to them being
one of the most sought-after Christmas gifts of the season.

How did the Frisbee get its name?

It goes back to the Frisbie Pie Company of New Haven, Connecticut, where some employees started tossing around the company's pie pan. Close to 300 million Frisbees have been made in their 40 years of production: That's more than 20,000 made every day. The first mass-produced flying disk was called Pluto Platter, but its name was soon changed to Frisbee after the company learned about the Frisbie pie-pan tossing. The first Frisbee tournament was held at Dartmouth University in 1954.

As you know, the Internet is much more than e-mail and search engines. Americans are using it to download and watch videos as well. In December 2009, nearly 178 million Internet users watched 33 billion online videos—about 1.1 billion every day. YouTube garnered 40 percent (13 billion) of the videos and Hulu was in second place with 3 percent, but that was with just 1 billion videos that month. In the overall breakdown, the 136 million YouTube viewers watched about 97 videos per viewer and Hulu viewers watched about 23 videos per viewer.

Air Force One isn't just the president's airplane; it's also a Nike sneaker.

More than 300,000 Nike Air Force 1s were sold every day in 2009. The all-white, low-cut version of the sneaker has been the bestselling sneaker in the United States since 2007. When it was released in 1982, the original Air Force 1 was the first basketball shoe to use Nike's Air technology. Designers have created nearly 1,700 versions of the shoe using a wide range of materials, from gold to crocodile skin.

The bestselling animated movie "threequel" ever is *Toy Story 3*. The movie was released on July 10, 2010, and in one month it made more than $920 million in worldwide sales. People were spending on average about $30 million a day to watch the movie. *Toy Story 3* surpassed the reigning champion of animated movies of all times, *Shrek 2*. It's now ranked fifth among the bestselling movies of all time, behind *Avatar*, *Titanic*, *The Lord of the Rings: The Return of the King*, and *Pirates of the Caribbean: Dead Man's Chest*.

Can a toy car cost more than a real car?

It can if it's a Hot Wheels. The ultimate car for any Hot Wheels collector is the hot pink Rear-Loader Beach Bomb. This Hot Wheels collectible was modeled after the 1969 Volkswagen minivan and has reportedly been sold for as much as $70,000. While no one knows exactly how many were made (several prototypes were made but were not offered to the public), only two are known to exist today. Each day more than 14,400 Hot Wheels cars are sold to more than 15 million Hot Wheels collectors and children everywhere.

Game consoles are getting smaller and more powerful every year.

When Sony released the new, slimmer PlayStation 3, it sold 1 million units in three weeks, which is 48,000 consoles every day. This version had 120GB hard drive that beats out the 40GB and 80GB hard drives of its predecessors. An extra bonus is that the PS3 can double—or triple— as a Blu-ray and DVD player. As of June 2010, PS3 owners can even play 3-D games through their PlayStations, provided they have 3-D TVs.

The largest music retail store is not a physical store, but an online store, iTunes.

In the first five months of 2008, the iTunes Store sold about 6.5 million songs every single day. By the end of June 2008, the iTunes Store had sold more than 5 billion songs. It took the store almost 3 years to sell their first billion songs, 10 months for the second billion songs, and 7 months for the third billion songs. The iTunes Store is now selling and renting movies. In 2008, the rate of movie downloads was 50,000 movies a day.

More than 95 million tweets are posted every day on Twitter. In a recent

Quantcast.com survey, several things were discovered about the tweets: 40 percent were useless babble, 37 percent were conversations, 6 percent were self-promotion, and about 3 percent were news. A Gizmodo survey found that out of every 100 tweeters, 5 people would be labeled loudmouths—the nickname for the small group who are responsible for 75 percent of all tweets.

Blu-ray Batman Bonanza! On the first day of sales, a record 600,000 copies of *The Dark Knight* were sold in the United States, Canada, and the United Kingdom. This high-definition video smashed the old record of 250,000 copies of *Iron Man* sold its first day. The pricier Blu-ray copy of *The Dark Knight* made up 20 percent of the total sales, and the number of copies sold the first week was a bat-rageous 1.7 million copies. The most recent Blu-ray top seller is *Avatar* with 1.5 million copies sold on its first day.

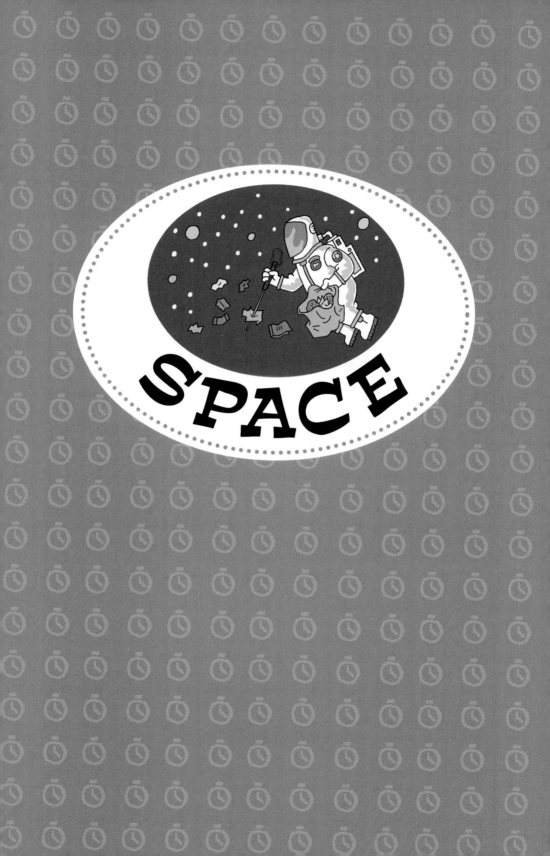

SPACE

Every day on Earth? How about half a year on Mercury?

On March 17, 2011, the space probe Mercury Messenger began its two-Mercury-day mission around the planet closest to our sun. Even more confusing: Those two "Mercury days" last a little over *four* "Mercury years." How is this possible? Mercury is a slow turner; it takes 176 Earth days to spin once on its axis. But since the tiny planet is so close to the sun, it takes just 88 Earth days to orbit around it. So, during Mercury Messenger's 12 Earth months orbiting Mercury, it will spend roughly two Mercury days, or four Mercury years, observing our solar system's smallest planet.

Every day on Earth there are 88 constellations in the sky, but you cannot see them all from one place.

If you live in the Northern Hemisphere, you can only see certain constellations, and others are visible only to people in the Southern Hemisphere. The constellations that the sun passes through during the year are the 13 constellations of the zodiac and can be seen by people in both hemispheres. The smallest constellation, with only four stars and 68 square degrees, is Crux, the Southern Cross. The largest is Hydra, with many bright stars and a span of more than 1,300 square degrees.

Can you image landing a spacecraft on an asteroid traveling 15 miles (24 kilometers) a second?

On February 12, 2001, NASA's Near Earth Asteroid Rendezvous Shoemaker spacecraft safely landed on the asteroid 433 Eros and was able to send data back to Earth. 433 Eros crosses the orbit of Mars and travels more than 1.3 million miles (2.1 million kilometers) every day. The landing is even harder to believe when you realize that this peanut-shaped asteroid is only 20.5 miles (33 kilometers) long and 8 miles (13 kilometers) wide, slightly larger than Manhattan Island.

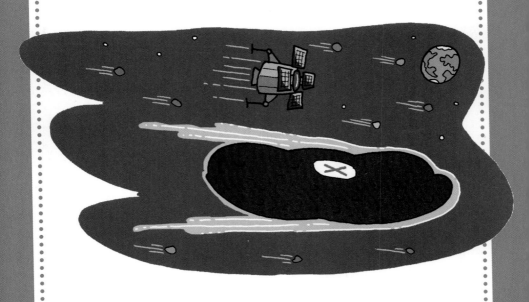

Do you ever fear that Earth might get sucked into a black hole someday? Not to worry, the closest black hole to us is 1,600 light-years away, and the closest supermassive (millions of times more massive than our sun) black hole is in the middle of the Milky Way galaxy. Our solar system is about 28,000 light-years away from it, on one of the outer arms of the Milky Way. Astronomers believe that there could be as many as 100 million black holes in our galaxy, but only about a dozen have been identified. In the entire visible universe of 100 billion galaxies, astronomers believe that 86,400 new black holes are being formed every day.

Even if you don't drive, you've probably heard of GPS (Global Positioning System), but how does it work?

Every day, about 12,550 miles (20,200 kilometers) above the Earth, there are 31 satellites sending information back to GPS receivers on Earth. The first GPS satellites were launched in 1978, using solar panels as a power source and nickel-cadmium batteries as a backup when traveling through the Earth's shadow.

How do you discover a comet without ever having seen it?

Probably the best-known comet in the world, Halley's comet was never seen by Edmund Halley, because he died 16 years before it appeared in the sky again. Halley studied one comet that seemed to appear every 76 years. In 1705 he predicted that the comet would appear in 1758—and it did. At its fastest speed, Halley's comet travels 2.9 million miles (4.7 million kilometers) a day. At its slowest, it covers more than 53,600 miles (86,400 kilometers) a day. Halley's comet will be seen from Earth again in 2061.

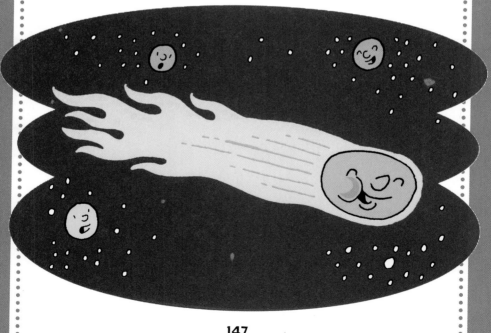

The Hubble Space Telescope sends 17 gigabytes of data back to Earth every day.

The Hubble was named after the astronomer Edwin Hubble, who was the first person to state that there were other galaxies in space beyond our Milky Way galaxy. The Hubble's main mirror is 94.5 inches (2.4 meters) in diameter, where ground-based telescopes can be 400 inches (1,000 centimeters) or more. But the Hubble can "see" much more clearly in space.

How many times did you sneeze today?

If you were an astronaut on the International Space Station (ISS), you'd be sneezing about 100 times a day. Are astronauts allergic to space? No—the dust inside the ISS does not settle down on surfaces, but constantly floats around instead, causing the astronauts to sneeze. Even with its floating dust, the ISS is more heavily shielded from outside dust and debris than any other spacecraft ever put into space.

What kind of phone is better than a cell phone?

A satellite phone can be used almost anywhere in the world and doesn't depend on cellular towers. Instead, it relies on orbiting satellites to send and receive signals every day. Iridium is one kind of satellite phone that uses scores of satellites to provide phone service. The Iridium satellite's antenna is highly reflective and produces bright flares, or glints, that can easily be seen from Earth if you look in the right place at the right time. The flares are up to 30 times brighter than Venus, can last from 5 to 20 seconds, and have even been seen during the daylight hours.

Believe it or not, there are "Goldilocks zones" in space. These are places not too close or too far away from a star, giving them a temperature that's "just right" for liquid water to exist. The Kepler spacecraft is currently scanning the Goldilocks zones of more than 100,000 stars every day. The onboard 0.95-meter Schmidt telescope has the largest camera ever sent into space attached to it.

What's a moon buggy?

"Moon Buggy" was the nickname given to the lunar rover that the astronauts drove on their moon missions. The lunar rover was able to top out at 11 miles (17.7 kilometers) per hour, which means it *could* have traveled 264 miles (425 kilometers) in one day. However, the longest trip of the three lunar rovers was just 17 miles (27.8 kilometers). There is an Annual Great Moonbuggy Race in Huntsville, Alabama, where students design a human-powered, two-person (one male and one female) vehicle that has to travel 0.7 mile (1.1 kilometers) on simulated lunar terrain with rocks, craters, and lunar soil.

Talk about extreme remote-controlled vehicles.

Technicians on Earth can control the movement of the Mars Rovers, Spirit and Opportunity, from an average distance of about 154 million miles (227 million kilometers). It takes the signal an average of 4 minutes to get to the vehicles from Earth. The rovers were designed to travel 44 yards (40 meters) in a single day and to cover a total distance of three-quarters of a mile (1 kilometer)—which they have since exceeded. The rovers are robotic geologists whose mission is to collect samples of rocks and soil. The rovers have also taken more than 100,000 pictures of the Red Planet.

How large are the meteors in a meteor shower?

Most of the meteors are no larger than a grain of sand, but the light they produce is visible from Earth. Larger particles can create real fireballs, much brighter and longer-lasting meteors. Even more spectacular is the bolide, in which the fireball's fragments and flares and sparks can be seen. The meteor shower that peaks every year around mid-December is the Geminids, which can produce from 1,920 to 2,400 meteors a day. Astronomers can predict the occurrence of meteor showers because the Earth's orbit crosses the paths of comet and asteroid trails at the same time every year.

If galaxies ate candy bars, Andromeda's favorite would be the Milky Way. The Andromeda galaxy is the nearest big spiral galaxy to our home galaxy, the Milky Way. The Andromeda galaxy looks like a smudge of light in the night sky, but it is actually almost twice the size of the Milky Way. While most galaxies are speeding away from each other, Andromeda and the Milky Way are getting 7.45 million miles (12 million kilometers) closer every day! Scientists predict that the galaxies will collide in about 3 billion years.

Have you ever heard of the far side of the moon?

That's because the moon only shows one side of itself—its near side—to Earth. The moon does rotate on its axis, but its rotation takes the same amount of time as its revolution around Earth, which is about 53,600 miles (86,400 kilometers) every day. Thus the far side of the moon is always hidden. Here's a way to demonstrate how the moon hides its far side: Ask someone to stand in the middle of a room. Place an object behind your back, and then slowly walk, turning as you do to keep that person from seeing the object. If you do this right, you should be able to go around the person without them seeing the object behind you.

A day the population of space reached 13.

On July 17, 2009, when space shuttle *Endeavour* reached the International Space Station, one galactic record was met while another was set. First, once *Endeavour* exited planet Earth, the fourteen-year-old record for the most humans in space was met: Its seven members joined the six other astronauts already floating around in the International Space Station. After *Endeavour* docked with the station and its crew climbed aboard the shuttle, a new record for the most humans aboard a single spacecraft while in outer space was set, making it a special day that was truly out of this world.

How many pieces of small space debris are orbiting the Earth every day?

There are about 19,000 objects larger than 3.9 inches (10 centimeters), an estimated 500,000 particles between 0.39 inches and 3.9 inches (1 and 10 centimeters), and tens of millions smaller than 0.39 inches (1 centimeter). This orbital debris is the result of collisions, explosions, solid rocket motor exhaust, and even tiny flecks of paint. The U.S. Space Surveillance Network keeps track of all particles larger than 3.9 inches (10 centimeters) and, using ground-based radar, can detect particles as small as three grains of sugar (0.11 inch, or 3 millimeters).

In 1967, graduate student Jocelyn Bell got the scare of her life.

She was examining a paper recording of static signals from the radio telescope she was using when all of a sudden, the static signal changed to steady pulses. She thought maybe it was an extraterrestrial trying to communicate with earthlings. Later, other astronomers determined that she had discovered a special neutron star called a pulsar that was spinning and giving off bursts of energy with each spin. There have been more than 1,800 pulsars discovered since that first one. Currently, the fastest-spinning pulsar (PSR J1748-2446ad) emits more than 61 million pulses every day.

How long is a day on Earth? Twenty-four

hours? Not quite. It is exactly 23 hours, 56 minutes, and 4 seconds. A day is calculated by the time it takes a planet to turn completely around on its axis. The planet Saturn has the second-shortest day of all the planets in our solar system, a day that was estimated to be 10 hours, 39 minutes, and 24 seconds in the 1980s. The Ulysses spacecraft flew by Saturn in the 1990s and calculated the day to be precisely 10 hours, 45 minutes, and 45 seconds.

Most people realize that the Earth is traveling 1,600,155 miles (2.5 million kilometers) around the sun every day, even if they don't sense the motion. However, our entire solar system is moving more than 1 million miles (1.6 million kilometers) a day toward the bright star **Vega** in the constellation Lyra. This velocity is not uncommon for the stars near the sun; it's basically the cruising speed of stars in our corner of the galaxy. Vega is about 25.3 light-years away from our solar system, so they will not be meeting anytime soon. Vega is the third-brightest star in the northern sky and the fifth brightest overall.

Most people know that the planets rotate on their axes, but few know that the sun also rotates on its axis. The sun rotates 4,467 miles (7,189 kilometers) per hour at its equator. Every day on Earth, the sun rotates 107,208 miles (172,536 kilometers). Since the sun is made of gases instead of solids, the area of the equator spins faster than the poles. The sun's equator makes a complete rotation in about 25 days, but it takes 36 days to completely rotate at the poles.

How would you like to drive a vehicle whose speedometer goes from zero to 2 miles (3.2 kilometers) per hour?

A space shuttle crawler is a vehicle that takes a space shuttle and its mobile launcher platform (MLP) to the launching pad. A crawler travels only 1 mile (1.6 kilometers) per hour when carrying the shuttle. At that rate, it would only go 24 miles (38.6 kilometers) in one day. However, the crawler only has to travel 3.5 miles (5.6 kilometers). A crawler is 131 feet (40 meters) long, 114 feet (35 meters) wide, and from 20 to 26 feet (6 to 8 meters) tall. The weight of a crawler, without the space shuttle and its **MLP**, is 6 million pounds (2.7 million kilograms).

Which would mess up your hair more, a stream of solar wind traveling at 1 million miles (1.6 million kilometers) per hour or a wind on Earth blowing 13 miles (21 kilometers) per hour?

The wind on Earth would mess up your hair more. The solar wind moves extremely fast, but it's made of so very few particles, it wouldn't have enough mass to move your hair. When traveling at its average speed, the solar wind will travel 24 million miles (38.4 million kilometers) in one day, which means it takes almost four days to go the 93 million miles (149.5 million kilometers) to the Earth.

When the sun has a spot on it, the spot is larger than most planets.

In 2010 the sun had an average of 41 sunspots, but that number changed daily. Sunspot activity goes in 11-year cycles of high and low numbers of sunspots. However, scientists are predicting that 2010–2011 will see one of the most intense sunspot cycles in the 400 years that records of sunspots have been kept. Scientists estimate there to be about 160 sunspots in total, plus or minus 25. Sunspots come in pairs and can usually last a few days, but the larger ones can last for a few weeks.

Who's got our back watching out for killer comets or asteroids?

Every day, the Pan-STARRS 1 telescope takes pictures of the night sky above Haleakala, on the Hawaiian Island of Maui. The telescope uses its 1,400 megapixel digital camera to map portions of the night sky, looking for moving objects heading for Earth. Every night, the camera takes more than 500 pictures, enough to fill 1,000 DVDs. The Pan-STARRS 1, with its 60-inch-diameter (1.5-meter-diameter) mirror, is just an experimental prototype of a new telescope planned for Mauna Kea in Hawaii with four times the power of Pan-STARRS 1.

"Exploding stars" isn't a reference to Hollywood.

There are stars in the universe that are blown apart by extremely strong forces within them. A nova is an exploding star, and a supernova is a gigantic exploding star of unimaginable proportions. Astronomers believe that there are countless supernova explosions every day in our universe. There has not been a supernova sighting in the Milky Way galaxy in centuries. The last Milky Way supernova was Kepler's supernova in October 1604. The closest supernova since then, named 1987A, was spotted in a nearby galaxy, the Large Magellanic Cloud, in 1987.

If you think the Earth has a lot of lightning strikes, you should try visiting Venus.

Wait, maybe you wouldn't want to visit there. Venus has an atmosphere of sulfuric acid, which wouldn't be very good for your health. Scientists believe that Venus has even more than the Earth's 8-million-plus lightning strikes a day. Unlike the Earth's water vapor–produced lightning, Venus's lightning comes from its sulfuric acid cloud base. Venus's surface is very hot and the atmospheric pressure is greater than the Earth's. Even though Mercury is closer to the sun, Venus is the hottest planet in our solar system—another reason *not* to visit.

Just how much heat energy does our sun give off every day?

Enough to evaporate nearly a trillion tons of water. Water in lakes, rivers, and oceans absorbs the heat energy; when the water molecules get heated to just the right temperature, they change into water vapor and rise up to form clouds. During this process, the evaporating water cools the lakes, rivers, and oceans, just like evaporating sweat cools your body. What would happen if Earth's surface weren't 72 percent covered in water? We'd have to find a new home. Earth would be way too hot to live on.

The latest innovation in TV is the 3-D set.

Thanks to South Korea's participation in the 2010 World Cup soccer games, Korea's two largest makers of flat-screen TVs, Samsung Electronics and LG Electronics, sold 9,000 3-D sets in June, just in South Korea alone. That's more than 300 3-D TVs a day! By the end of 2010, Samsung planned to sell more than 26 million additional 3-D TVs at home and around the world, which figures to be more than 142,000 sets a day. Watching 3-D soccer could be scary when the ball seems to be coming out of the TV set, but it's got to be better than watching 3-D boxing!

Why is it called a Blu-ray player?

The Blu-ray player uses a "blue laser" to read the optical disc instead of the red laser that's used to read a standard DVD. The blue laser's light is not exactly blue to the human eye— it's purple. A Blu-ray disc can store about 10 times more data than a standard DVD disc. More people are using Blu-ray players every day. Over 30,000 a day were sold in 2010. The double-layer Blu-ray disc can hold an incredible 50GB of data. And 3-D Blu-ray discs are now on the horizon.

Did you get that fax? More than 550 million

sheets of paper are faxed on an average day in the United States.
The latest trend in faxing is paperless faxing, where the original
is emailed to the person and the data is stored electronically.
More than 1 million trees would be saved if just 5 percent of all
faxes were paperless. That same amount of paperless faxing
would also save an estimated 360 million gallons (1.36 billion
liters) of water and 215 million kilowatt-hours of electricity, and
eliminate 3 million pounds (1.4 million kilograms) of air pollution.

Ever see a dinosaur? The VCR is a technological "dinosaur" compared to the DVR. Digital video recorders have a hard drive like a computer, but it's many times larger. They can store more than 80 hours of recordings whereas VCRs could only record up to 10 hours on one tape. More than 28.1 million DVRs were sold in 2009, which is more than 76,900 DVRs a day. According to one survey, the DVR ranks third behind the washing machine (#1) and microwave oven (#2) as the most indispensable item in a person's home.

On the day before Thanksgiving, it's estimated that there are 2.3 million people flying to eat their turkeys.

That's a lot of people in the airports and in the air at the same time. Sometimes, snow and winter storms can delay and cancel flights. In the coming years, Travelocity plans to have spotters at the 12 busiest airports and will be doing live Twitter updates two days before Thanksgiving.

Will robots ever take over the world?

Robot comes from the Czech word *robota*, which means "slavelike" or "drudgery work." There are about 140,000 robots now working every day in the manufacturing business alone. At first, most were found in automobile manufacturing plants, where robots welded and painted cars and trucks. Today robots are found in many industries, including aerospace, consumer goods, food, and pharmaceuticals. An American, Joe Engelberger, was called the father of robotics. He created the first industrial robot, called Unimate.

Apparently, everyone but mall cops missed the revolution.

Once billed as an invention to revolutionize personal transportation, the Segway Human Transporter failed to gain traction among consumers. Only 30,000 Segways scooted off salesroom floors in six years. That's only about 14 Segways a day. Amazingly, the Segway operates without an engine, brakes, or a steering wheel. It has a rechargeable battery that is powerful enough to provide two hours of riding on just one hour of charging.

Coal mining has changed from the days when miners used pickaxes and shovels.

Today about 31 percent of underground mines use a massive machine called a longwall. In the United States, more than 100 longwalls are used underground, mainly in the Appalachia region. A regular longwall can chew away over 13,000 tons (12,000 metric tons) of coal a day, while a high-performance longwall can cut away 29,000 tons (26,000 metric tons) in a day. How much coal is 29,000 tons? A West Virginia power plant consumes 26,000 tons (23,600 metric tons), generating enough power for 2 million homes.

Don't throw that battery away! Nearly

8 million batteries are thrown away in the United States every single day. Most end up in landfills, where they can cause unnecessary pollution by leaking and releasing heavy metals that could make their way to groundwater systems. On average, American homes have 21 battery-operated devices, but only one home out of six recycles batteries. Today, rechargeable batteries are available and can be recharged over and over to save money and the environment. New rechargeable batteries can now be recharged in less than two hours, some in an hour or less.

What's more spectacular than an Independence Day fireworks display?

In 2008, individual Americans bought more than 186.4 million pounds (84.5 million kilograms) of the pyrotechnic devices, while cities bought an additional 26.8 million pounds (12.1 million kilograms). That's a total of 213 million pounds (96.6 million kilograms), or 584,109.5 pounds (264,947.6 kilograms) a day! But it's not like that many are sold every day. About 90 percent of all fireworks sold in a year are sold during the first week of July.

The world's largest hydroelectric plant is the Three Gorges Dam, located on the Yangtze River in China. In the later part of 2008, the plant was producing 18,300 megawatts of electricity every day. That's a lot, but even more when you consider 1 megawatt equals 1 *million* watts! Twenty-six generators are currently operating, with six more to become fully operational in 2011. When all the generators are working, they will produce 22,500 megawatts every day, which is currently one-tenth of the total Chinese demand for electricity. The Three Gorges Dam stands 607 feet (185 meters) high and 7,575 feet (1.4 miles, or 2,309 meters) wide.

Where does a Nimitz-class aircraft carrier store the freshwater it needs for a crew of 5,000 sailors? It doesn't.

It makes its own water with its onboard desalination plant. In one day, the plant can change 400,000 gallons (1,500,000 liters) of ocean salt water into clean freshwater, which equals the usage of 2,000 average American homes. The nuclear-powered aircraft carrier is full of amazing features: One anchor weighs in at 30 tons (27 tonnes); it carries enough food for 6,000 people for around 70 days; it has a medical staff of 6 doctors and 5 dentists; and in an average week the barber (yep, only one barber) gives more than 1,500 haircuts.

Indianapolis 500 race cars use ethanol, a kind of alcohol, for fuel.

America is the largest ethanol-producing country, with a daily total of 35 million gallons (133 million liters), made from corn and grain sorghum. Brazil ranks second in the production of ethanol, and most of its ethanol is made from sugarcane. The most promising kind of ethanol produced is cellulosic ethanol, made using the cellulose found in plant cells. The source of the cellulose can be fast-growing trees and grasses and even crop wastes like rice straw, corn stover (leaves, stalks, and cobs left in the field after harvest), and wood chips.

Who says the desert is a wasteland?

The largest solar photovoltaic power plant is located on 140 acres (56 hectares) in the desert of southern Nevada, at Nellis Air Force Base. The plant uses 72,000 solar panels to produce 68,490 kilowatt-hours of electricity every day. The solar panels use a solar tracking system that follows the sun across the sky to get the maximum amount of solar radiation. Today, the 12,000 workers and residents on the air base acquire 25 percent of their electrical power from the plant. The plant saves the air force $1 million every year and reduces carbon dioxide emissions for the rest of us.

Humankind has come a long way from the pencil and pad of paper to Apple's newest creation, the iPad. People must really want their iPads, because more than 37,500 were purchased every day in the first 80 days they went on sale. The iPad is like a handheld computer without the keyboard and bulky parts. It's lighter and thinner than all the laptops and netbooks on the market today. All the user has to do is touch the Multi-Touch screen to type, search, zoom, scroll, or perform any number of other functions. The iPad can also use all the apps developed for the iPhone and iPod.

Would you pay $30,000 to rent *Alvin* for one day?

No, not the singing chipmunk, but the world's first deep-sea-diving submersible able to carry passengers—usually a pilot and two observers. *Alvin* is propelled by five hydraulic thrusters; its cruising speed is 1 knot (1.85 kilometers per hour), with a maximum speed of 2 knots (3.7 kilometers per hour). Every year, *Alvin* makes between 150 and 200 dives—that's the equivalent of about half a dive a day. One of its most famous dives was to locate a hydrogen bomb lost from a B-52 that collided with a tanker plane. *Alvin* also made 12 dives to the RMS *Titanic* to take photos of the sunken ocean liner.

An electric sports car? Yep. The Tesla Motors company has created just that, the Roadster 2.5. This electric racer can out-accelerate most gasoline-powered sports cars on the market today, and it does it without producing harmful emissions. Since Tesla first started making cars in 2008, roughly two new cars are sold on an average day. The Roadster plugs into just about any electrical outlet anywhere in the world and can travel 245 miles (394 kilometers) on a single charge. With a top speed of 125 miles (201 kilometers) per hour, how far could it travel in a day—and how many times would it have to charge?

People are crazy about their smartphones and can't wait to get their hands on the latest version. When the Apple iPhone 4 was released, the preorders reached more than 600,000 in a single day. During the first three days it was released, it sold 1.7 million phones—that's 566,666 every day—making it the bestselling iPhone in history. According to Steve Jobs, one of the owners of Apple, the iPhone 4 has more than 100 new features compared to its predecessor, the iPhone 3G. Three new versions of the iPhone have come in the last three years.

Farm animals in the United States are producing about 2.8 million tons (2.5 metric tons) of poop every day! Scientists and engineers have designed things called anaerobic digesters that can "digest" the waste and produce methane gas. All of that methane could be used to generate enough electricity to power thousands of homes and businesses. Animal poop is no longer a waste, but an important source of renewable energy. One Minnesota farmer is using manure from his 900 cows to produce methane gas to generate enough electricity for his entire farm and 70 other homes. Each of his cows produces 100 pounds (45 kilograms) of poop every day.

Guess how many ships pass through the Panama Canal on an average day?

If you said 40 ships, you're right! It takes most ships 12 hours to travel the 50-mile (80-kilometer) stretch from the Atlantic to the Pacific Ocean. Passing through the canal saves ships from going an extra 8,000 nautical miles (15,000 kilometers). The canal is open 24 hours a day for the entire year. In the 1880s, the French were the first to try to construct the canal; they lost 22,000 men in their failed attempt. The Americans lost thousands of men as well, but completed the canal in 1914.

What makes a smartphone smart?

It can do so much more than make calls; most have the hardware and software of a computer, which allows you to surf the Web, send and receive e-mails, and check where you are with a built-in GPS. More than 476,164 smartphones were sold every day across the planet in 2009. But they were outsold by the regular phone, which sold at a rate of about 2.8 million phones a day. Currently, about one in five Americans has a smartphone. However, some experts believe that by the end of 2011, one in two Americans will have one.

Can you imagine about half of New York City covered with wind turbines?

That's the size of the largest wind farm in America. This giant farm near Roscoe, Texas, covers nearly 100,000 acres (40,500 hectares) and has 627 wind turbines with a capacity of 781.5 megawatts of electricity. They produce enough daily to power 250,000 average-size Texas homes. Texas leads the nation with 9,707 megawatts of wind power, followed by Iowa with its 3,670 megawatts. A California company is planning a 1,500-megawatt addition to the wind farm in Tehachapi Pass. When completed, it will be the largest single wind farm in the country.

What would the world be without computers?

More than a billion people would probably be upset, because there were a billion computers in use at the end of 2008. More than 780,000 new computers are produced every day. It took about 27 years for the first billion computers to be sold in the world but only 7 years to reach the second billion. Not all the computers that have been made are being used; most people are probably on their fourth or fifth computer right now.

People said that it couldn't be done.

But the impossible has been accomplished: A solar-powered airplane, called Solar Impulse, flew for one 24-hour day without landing. It accomplished this feat near Bern, Switzerland, on July 7, 2010. During the daylight hours, the plane's 12,000 solar cells provided electricity to power the plane's four motors and to charge the onboard batteries used during the night. The plane was piloted by André Borschberg, and it had the same wingspan as a Boeing 777 passenger jet. The solar plane ascended to 28,000 feet (8,535 meters) and flew more than 43 miles (70 kilometers) per hour.

During a standard 90-minute soccer match, the average player runs a distance of about 6.2 miles (10 kilometers). That would be like running the length of an **NBA** court 350 times! If that same player were to compete in an all-day game—a fútbol fanatic's dream—he or she would run about 99.2 miles (159.6 kilometers). But he or she would probably be way too tired to score any goals, because running that far would be like running from New York City to Philadelphia in a single day!

Would you ride on a "Snurfer"? The

very first snowboard was a skateboard with a leash and without
the wheels. It was developed in the 1960s and was called a
"Snurfer." Snowboarders all over the world spend more than $1.3
million on snowboards every day. There are more than 6 million
snowboarders, and the number is increasing daily. Snowboarding
has been an Olympic sport since 1998, now with three events
for men and three for women. Shaun White is probably the best-
known snowboarder in the world and has won two Olympic gold
medals in the half-pipe competitions.

A marathon a day . . .

As a child, Stefaan Engels suffered from asthma and was told he would not be able to play sports, but on February 5, 2011, Stefaan completed his 365th marathon in Barcelona, Spain, by running a 26.2-mile (42.2-kilometer) marathon every day for one year. The journey began in his hometown of Ghent, Belgium, and he traveled a total of 9,569 miles (15,401 kilometers) in marathons in the United States, Portugal, Canada, Mexico, and Great Britain. Stefaan's best time for the marathons was 2 hours and 56 minutes, but he averaged an incredible 4 hours for each race. Stefaan did the feat to inspire others to take the time to exercise in their busy schedules. By the time he finished his feat, he had gone through 25 pairs of shoes!

Can you name an American sport that was once played on a field from 1 to 15 miles (1.6 to 24 kilometers) long; had as many as 1,000 players on a side; used a ball made of wood, stone, baked clay, or deerskin; and sometimes took days to finish?

According to legend, these were characteristics of the style of lacrosse early **Native Americans** played. **Every** day in America, there are more than 250,000 lacrosse players from second grade to college. Lacrosse is **played by both boys and girls** in 2,000 high schools and 600 colleges.

What takes 75 days to make but only lasts one day?

It's a cricket ball. A cricket ball is made with a cork-rubber ball at its center. The core is covered with narrow sheets of cork and wet wool string. Then it's beaten into a sphere with a wooden mallet. After the ball dries, the same process is repeated four more times, which can take two and a half months to complete. Finally, the ball is covered with leather and sewn together with between 78 and 82 stitches. After a day of getting tossed and whacked around by professional cricket players, its meticulous design is not enough to keep it from being misshaped to the point it can no longer be used.

What's that *hmmmmmm* noise?

Apparently, vuvuzela ear is one of the side effects of World Cup fever. A stadium full of these plastic noisemakers can produce 140 decibels of droning. That's louder than a plane taking off! However, the noisemakers were a moneymaker for the Johannesburg-based **Vuvuzela Branding Company**, whose sales went from 20,000 a month to 20,000 a day in the two weeks leading up to the 2010 World Cup in South Africa. So, who's to blame? More than 70 percent of the sales went to fans from the United Kingdom, Brazil, and Portugal.

During the first month of its release, *Madden NFL 2009* sold a bone-crushing 2.3 million copies. That's just over 74,193 copies every day! Luckily for all those rushing to play, the infamous "Madden Curse" only applies to the players on the cover. Whether the curse is real or not, since players first began appearing on the video game's cover in 1999, nine players have seen a drastic decline in their performance (usually after suffering serious injury) the year they appeared on the cover.

About 1,370,000 rounds of golf are played every day in America. But since a round of golf can be played by between one and four golfers, the actual number of *golfers* out there putting around every day swings between 1,370,000 and 5,480,000. Sure, it's every golfer's dream to hit a hole in one, but those are some pretty big dreams: Official holes in one occur only once every 3,500 rounds—that's about 400 every day. Feeling lucky? Forget holes in one at the 17th hole of TPC Sawgrass in Florida. The hole's so tricky, an average of 329 golf balls are lost in the water surrounding it every day.

Believe it or not, the average cost of a 30-second Super Bowl commercial actually went down in 2010. And it was the first time since 2006–2007 that the cost of an ad during the big game dipped. So, how big of a discount did advertisers get for Super Bowl XLIV? The average cost was $2.5–$2.8 million dollars for a 30-second ad—down from a $3 million average price tag on ads for the previous Super Bowl. So, if you really hate Super Bowl Sunday and wish you could have a day without football, it would only cost you about $7.2–$8.1 billion to take out a full-day commercial to play instead of the game.

Vroom! Vroom! There go the **NASCAR** cars, speeding around the track. But what if they could travel on a highway at that speed for one day? How many miles would they go? It depends on the racetrack. The fastest track is Talladega Superspeedway, where the average speed is 188 miles (303 kilometers) per hour. Driving 188 miles per hour for 24 hours would take a person 4,512 miles (7,261 kilometers). A person could travel from San Diego, California, to Jacksonville, Florida, and back to San Diego in one day if they drove in a straight line. But that only allows 16 total minutes for pit stops, both bathroom and gassing up.

The longest single-day stage at the 2010 Tour de France was Stage 6, with a total distance of 141.4 miles (227.5 kilometers). The top racer that day was Mark Cavendish, with a time of 5 hours, 37 minutes, and 42 seconds, but the top story was the fight at the end of the race. After Spanish cyclist Carlos Barredo thought Portuguese cyclist Rui Costa had elbowed him during the race, Barredo attacked Costa with a wheel from his bike. The two fell to the ground, fists flying. As punishment, the cyclists were fined about $380 for inappropriate behavior.

Do you think you could outrun a horse?

Of course not, but could Usain Bolt, the planet's fastest person? Still not even close. While Bolt can fly like lighting at 23.7 miles (38.2 kilometers) per hour, he wouldn't come close to Secretariat. Widely considered to be the fastest racehorse of all time, Secretariat was clocked at 37.5 miles (60 kilometers) per hour in the 1973 Belmont Stakes. He finished the 1.5-mile (2.4-kilometer) race in just 2 minutes and 24 seconds. If he were to keep up that pace for a full day, he could run 900 miles (1,440 kilometers) in a day.

Competing in the "world's toughest footrace," runners in the Badwater Ultramarathon hoof it 135 miles (217 kilometers), all under the 2-day time limit for the race. That means even the race's "slowest" finishers still run an average of 67.5 miles (108.5 kilometers) every day during the race. But the distance isn't this race's only challenge. Heat and elevation also factor in. The race is held each year in mid-July to ensure the desert temperatures are at their peak—up to 125° Fahrenheit (52.2° Celsius)—and the course winds from a start of 282 feet (86 meters) below sea level up to a final height of 8,300 feet (2,530 meters) above sea level!

On the first Saturday of March, dozens of humans and over 1,000 dogs line up for one of the longest races in the world, the Iditarod Trail Sled Dog Race. Each team of 12 to 16 dogs pulls its musher (the person riding the dogsled) through the cold Alaskan wilderness in this race from Anchorage to Nome, Alaska. The course is about 1,112 miles (1,789 kilometers) long on even years, and 1,131 miles (1,820 kilometers) long on odd years. The fastest time was 8 days, 22 hours, 46 minutes, and 2 seconds, set in 2002 by Martin Buser. That means Buser and his dogs covered just under 125 miles (201 kilometers) every day during the race. The race's slowest winning time was set by Carl Huntington with 20 days, 15 hours, 2 minutes, and 7 seconds in 1974.

Believe it or not, Iron Man isn't just a movie character.

In fact, there are thousands of Ironmen—and Ironwomen—all over the world. What does it take to become a "real" Ironman? You've got to be able to complete a three-part race: a 2.4-mile (3.86-kilometer) swim, a 112-mile (180.25-kilometer) bike ride, and a full marathon (26.2 miles, or 42.2 kilometers) to finish. In order to pull this feat off, participants burn anywhere from 6,000 to 8,000 calories during the race. That's three to four times more calories than the average person burns every day without exercise.

From 1970 to 1999, hockey player Wayne Gretzky netted an astounding 2,857 points. What's even more amazing is that he did so in just 1,487 games. Since he only played one game a day, that means he scored nearly 2 points every game day of his playing career. Just how many points is 2,857? The number-two player on the all-time hockey points list, Mark Messier, has only 1,887 points—and it took him 1,756 games to score them.

Even when it's not game day, the Indianapolis Colts' celebrity quarterback, Peyton Manning, scores an average of $38,371.84 every day. That's only slightly under the average *yearly* personal income in America. And while quarterbacks are often tossed around by oversized brutes, Manning's job has been the cushiest in the league. He was sacked a league low of 10 times. That's less than once a game. This is not to say Manning isn't a hard worker; only Brett Favre has played more consecutive games (285) than Manning's 192. In fact, Manning has started every single game since he has been in the league.

In baseball, players think safety when they think base.

You might have other thoughts if you were to ever try **BASE** jumping. **BASE** is an acronym for everything **BASE** jumpers throw themselves off of: buildings, antennas, spans (bridges or any other structure spanning a chasm), and earth (cliffs, canyons, and mountains). Sounds so crazy, who would want to do this? In 2009, at West Virginia's New River Gorge Bridge Day, 800 jumpers took the plunge from the 876-foot-high (267-meter-high) bridge.

There are literally millions of children playing Rock Paper Scissors every day. While the exact origins of this game of skill, chance, and decision are murky, it is widely played on every continent. Traditionally, the game has been used to settle disputes; more recently the game has been played to settle championships. For the past six years, hundreds of "hand athletes" compete for the RPS World Championship title. If you're thinking of putting your hand in the ring, you might want to practice. Inventor Steve Hoefer has recently come up with an RPS training glove. It's an electronic glove capable of playing Rock Paper Scissors against its wearer.

During the final match of the FIFA 2010 World Cup in South Africa between Spain and the Netherlands, there were an estimated 700 million soccer fanatics worldwide watching for the day. In the United States alone, an estimated 24.3 million people tuned in, making it the most watched soccer match in U.S. history. Those numbers are strong, but that's less than 10 percent of the U.S. population. Champion Spain, on the other hand, had nearly 17 million watching—that's 91 percent of the country's total television audience!

217

Source Notes

About.com
AbsoluteAstronomy.com
Air & Space (magazine)
Air Info Now
Alamo Colleges
All Koalas
American Academy of Family Physicians
American Foundation for Children with
    Cancer
American Mosquito Control Association
American Pet Products Association
American Pyrotechnics Association
American Wind Energy Association
*Animal Planet: The Most Extreme
    Bugs,* Animal Planet
Annenberg Learner
Answerbag
Apple Inc.
Arbor Day Foundation
Arco Aluminum
Arizona-Sonora Desert Museum
ARKive
associatedcontent.com
Astronomical Society of the Pacific
Astronomy (magazine)
Atlanta Fulton County Zoo
Autoblog Green
Bat Conservation International
BBC
best-ever-cookie-collection.com
Beverage Marketing Corporation
Bicycling (magazine)
Big Fish Diving
Biofuel Industry Today
Black Pearl Gallery
Bloomberg Businessweek
Bloomberg.com
Blu-ray.com
brainhealthandpuzzles.com
Bright Hub
Brookline Youth Lacrosse
California Walnut Commission
CampSilos
Can Manufacturers Institute
Canadian Association of Wound Care
Case Western Reserve University

CBS News
Center for Ecoliteracy
Chicago Tribune
China Coal Resource
Chinese Society for Rock Mechanics
    and Engineering
Chipotle Mexican Grill
Clean Air Council
Cleveland Clinic
CNN
Coconut Research Center
Colorado School of Mines
Columbia University
Complete Bamboo
Conservation Report
Contactmusic.com
Cotton Incorporated
countrymusic.about.com
CrunchBase
CSGNetwork.com
CTIA: The Wireless Association
Daily Mail (U.K.)
Dave's Cool Toys
DesertUSA.com
Diamondfacts.org
Diaper Industry Source
didyouknow.org
Digital Entertainment Group
Discover (magazine)
Discovery Channel
Earth911.com
eHow
EnchantedLearning.com
Encyclopedia of Life
ESPN
Eurogamer Network
European Day of Languages
Eye Health Vision Centers
FaxtoEmailGuide.com
FitDay
Food and Agriculture Organization
    of the United Nations
FoodNavigator.com
FoodReference.com
Forbes
Fox News

Simple Ecology
Skyrider for Kids
SmartPlanet
Smithsonian Institution
Smithsonian National Zoological Park
Snowboarding Zone
Solar Impulse
Space Exploration, DK Eyewitness Books
Space.com
Spaceweather.com
SparkPeople
Squidoo
Star Tribune (Minnesota)
Strategy Analytics
suite101.com
Sundia Corp
Sunkist Growers
Swiss Gastro-Intestinal Center
TechCrunch
Termites Gone Wild
Tesla Motors
Texas A&M University
Texas Oncology
The Incredible Machine, National Geographic
Tiger Foundation
Time (magazine)
Toms Shoes
Topend Sports Network
Travel & Leisure
TravelMath.com
Troyer Farms
TWICE: This Week in Consumer Electronics
Unclaimed Baggage Center
Understanding Nutrition, Eleanor Noss
    Whitney & Sharon Rady Rolfes
United Mine Workers of America
United Nations Educational, Scientific and
    Cultural Organization
United Press International
Universe Today
University of Colorado Boulder
University of Florida
University of Illinois
University of Miami
University of Michigan Museum of Zoology
University of Minnesota
University of Missouri
University of New Mexico
University of South Australia

University of Southern California
U.S. Census Bureau
U.S. Department of Labor
U.S. Environmental Protection Agency
U.S. Grains Council
U.S. News & World Report
U.S. Sugar Corporation
USA Rugby
USA Today
USA Track & Field
Virginia Apple Growers Association
Vuvuzela Branding Co.
Wall Street Journal
*Warman's Hot Wheels Field Guide: Values
    and Identification*, Michael Zarnock
Warner Bros. Entertainment
Washington University in St. Louis
Water Encyclopedia
WebMD
Whipnet Technologies
White Castle Management Co.
whitehouse.gov
Whole Foods Market
WireUpdate
Wisconsin National Primate Research Center
Woman's Day
Worldometers.info
Worldwatch Institute
Yahoo!
ZDNet
Zeecric.com
Zegrahm Expeditions
ZhuZhu Pets
Zoological Society of San Diego

Index